ARCHES

NATIONAL PARK

WHERE ROCK
MEETS SKY
BY
NICKY LEACH

SIERRA PRESS
MARIPOSA, CA

DEDICATION

I dedicate this book to Castle Valley writer Terry Tempest Williams, whose life's work celebrating and defending the Redrock Country of southern Utah—through civic actions as well as fine prose—is as inspiring as the land itself. Ed Abbey would be well pleased!　　　　　　　　　—N.L.

ACKNOWLEDGMENTS

Any journey in Canyon Country is as much a journey into self as it is into landscape. This new book on Arches is no exception. My appreciation to the following people for accompanying me into the field, sharing stories, and expanding my vision: Arches National Park Chief of Interpretation Diane Allen and Southeast Utah Parks Chief of Interpretation Paul Henderson for taking time out of busy schedules to review my manuscript, ranger Murray Shoemaker for help with Arches' human history, and Miriam Graham, an enjoyable trail companion and fellow music lover; Brad Wallis, former executive director of Canyonlands Natural History Association, whose friendship, insights, and constant, quiet support I value highly; and US Geological Survey biologist Tim Graham and family, who made a trip into the Arches backcountry the most pleasurable and interesting Labor Day excursion ever. Back home, I am grateful to editor and valued friend Cindy Bohn for helping cross the T's and dot the I's. Last, but never least, my appreciation to photographer and publisher Jeff Nicholas, whose creative vision and wonderful spirit is woven into every part of the beautiful book you hold in your hands.—N.L.

FRONT COVER
Delicate Arch, late afternoon.
PHOTO ©RANDY PRENTICE
INSIDE FRONT COVER
Turret Arch seen through North Window.
PHOTO ©GEORGE H.H. HUEY
TITLE PAGE
The La Sal Mountains seen through Delicate Arch.
PHOTO ©STEVE MULLIGAN
PAGE 4/5
Courthouse Towers seen from upper Park Avenue.
PHOTO ©TOM TILL
PAGE 4 (BELOW)
Inside Double Arch, the Windows Section.
PHOTO ©ROBERT HILDEBRAND
PAGE 6/7
Balanced Rock with Venus and crescent Moon.
PHOTO ©JACK DYKINGA
PAGE 7 (LOWER RIGHT)
Inside South Window, Windows Section.
PHOTO ©JEFF D. NICHOLAS

4

CONTENTS

A PARALLEL WORLD

Fins of Entrada sandstone in Devils Garden. PHOTO ©RANDALL K. ROBERTS

Don't step lightly in the wildwood because a
government agency or a book tells you to do so.
Tread lightly out of affection, out of respect,
out of a generosity of spirit toward the land
and its wild inhabitants.
                    —David Foreman, EarthFirst!

It's an unusually cool summer's morning in Arches National Park. Heavy monsoon rains the day before have broken southeastern Utah's unprecedented drought conditions and washed away the dust of the last six months. High clouds stipple the soft blue sky. To the east is 12,000-foot Mount Tukuhnikivats, one of the highest summits in the La Sal Mountains. Its name means "where the sun lingers" in the Ute language. I wonder what names native people had for the landmarks in Arches. Did they, like the Navajo, believe the rocks in their homeland were once alive?

A breath of wind exhales gently over the high desert of the Paradox Basin. Still moist from the rainstorm, the great rolling plateau of eroded Entrada Sandstone seems to glow from within. It is a vibrant artist's palette: salmon, vermilion, ochre, buckskin. The colors of the desert.

What would New Mexico artist Georgia O'Keeffe have made of this landscape, I wonder? A lover of elemental forms and sensual textures, O'Keeffe would surely have been fascinated by the thousands of keyholes, windows, spans, and hoodoos at Arches. Whole canvases could be filled with flying buttresses of stone, framed mountain views, junipers clinging to sandstone, the enormous white trumpets of sacred datura at dawn. I can imagine sculptor Henry Moore, whose pale, holed, abstracted sculptures dot verdant British hills, peering through Double Arch and murmuring appreciatively over the clever use of "negative space," then returning to his studio reinspired.

Artists filter the natural world through the lens of their unique perceptions. Landscapes are never just landscapes but a human experience of what is there—as individual as a fingerprint. Nature is the artist here, though. Working in the medium of sandstone,

using the twin chisels of water and flowing underground salt, she uplifts, collapses, sculpts, and molds. Landscape is a work-in-progress, a performance art piece that is never finished—and therein lies its very perfection.

Artist Christo wraps up whole landscapes, giftwrapping them for us as if we were Christmas shoppers. Everywhere we turn, Delicate Arch is being used to sell something in our consumer society. Fortunately, Delicate Arch and the other rock landmarks at Arches cut through all our preconceived notions and still have the power, as Edward Abbey put it, "to startle the senses and surprise the mind out of its ruts of habit."

In this overscaled Zen rock garden, rocks balance precariously on pedestals. Massive sandstone arches are so impossibly slender, only a wing and a prayer seem to hold them up. Cliffs tilt at steep angles like dominoes caught in a slow-motion freefall. Our photographs may freeze-frame Delicate Arch, Landscape Arch, and the 2,000 other known arches in Arches, but in life they are always changing. Gravity is constantly at work on the exposed fins, taking down, grain by grain, 200 million years of sedimentation, lithification, uplift, and erosion. Sandstone to sand, dust to dust. All things must pass—even our most cherished landmarks. This is as it should be.

At 10 a.m., I arrive in the parking lot of the Fiery Furnace for a three-hour hike with Ranger Miriam Graham. While another ranger guides a tour, she will be roaming the jumble of sandstone fins, checking on climbing groups and backcountry hikers with permits who have elected to explore on their own. These occasional unfettered moments in a park ranger's busy day offer some of its greatest pleasures. Like many rangers, Miriam leads a full life. After work today, she will head home to a second job: tuning the pianos of world-class musicians at the annual Moab Music Festival.

We enter the Fiery Furnace, walking in washes and on slickrock to avoid cryptobiotic crust, the dark biological soil alive with the cyanobacteria, lichens, and algae that form the building blocks of life in the desert. The twisted branches of ancient shaggy

Entrada Sandstone fins of the Fiery Furnace.

junipers point the way at the junction of parallel canyons. They begin to look alike. I'm glad that Miriam is familiar with this maze. Life narrows down into a pleasing rhythm of one boot in front of the other, heartbeats and breath. I feel completely in the moment, all memories and future plans on hold. How simple it is to be happy, I think.

Beneath Skull Arch, we stop and eat trail mix, drink water, and sit for a while in companionable silence. I write notes in my journal. Miriam's radio crackles. We watch as clouds give way to blue sky through the eye sockets of the arch. Beyond the Fiery Furnace, the temperature is climbing. Inside here, it's cool and protected. In a neighboring corridor, we can hear a group of climbers calling to each other. Miriam winks at me, takes out her wooden Indian flute, and begins to play a haunting refrain. The voices suddenly go quiet.

As we leave, we come upon the strewn backpacks of the climbers. In a moment of playfulness, we debate hiding the packs behind a huge rock before our better judgment prevails. We settle for moving the equipment tidily to one side. But I can't resist having one last bit of fun. I tear a sheet of paper out of my note-

Petroglyphs near Wolfe Cabin.

book and, remembering the ancient flute player whose hump-backed form is found on canyon walls throughout the Southwest, I write KOKOPELLI WAS HERE. Then, laughing, we continue on our way—back to the real world.

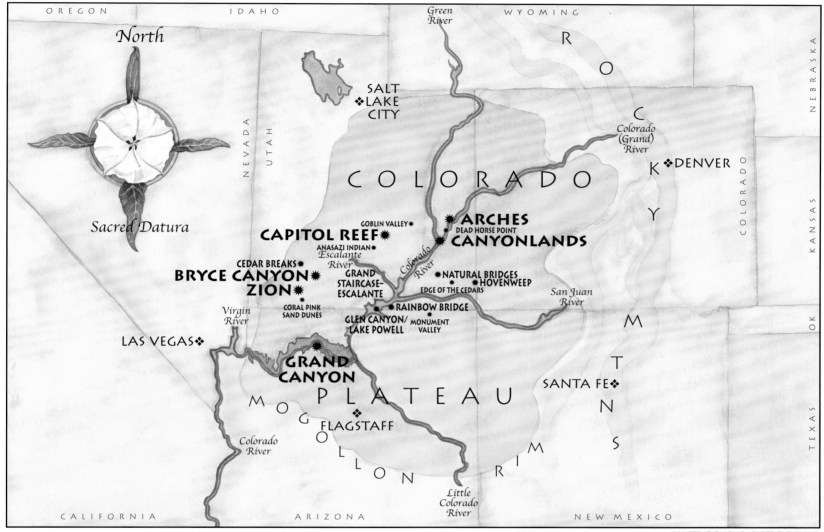

ILLUSTRATION BY DARLECE CLEVELAND

Arches National Park is located on the spectacular 130,000-square-mile, mile-high physiographic province known as the Colorado Plateau, home to the greatest concentration of national and state parks, national forests, Bureau of Land Management lands, wilderness areas, and Indian reservations in the nation.

Arches' undeveloped neighbor to the south, 527-square-mile Canyonlands National Park, offers exceptional backcountry explorations. The park is split into three units—Island in the Sky, the Needles, and the Maze—separated from each other by the Colorado and Green Rivers, which carved the labyrinthian canyons that form the heart of Canyon Country. This is rugged, undeveloped country. Don't travel here without first checking in with rangers. Carry topo maps, food, a gallon of water per person per day, extra tires, and roadside emergency repair equipment in all units. Canyonlands may also be entered from the river. Contact outfitters in Moab and Green River.

South of the Needles District of Canyonlands is Natural Bridges National Monument, which preserves three water-cut spans across a tributary of the Colorado River. To reach the park, drive west on Utah 95, a spectacular road that winds over Comb Ridge above the San Juan River and passes ancient Indian ruins and Grand Gulch Primitive Area, then crosses Lake Powell and Glen Canyon National Recreation Area.

The USDA Forest Service and Bureau of Land Management offer good alternatives to busy parks in the high season. When summer temperatures hit the 100s, Manti-La Sal National Forest, spread between the La Sal Mountains east of Moab and the Abajo Mountains west of Monticello, offers cool hiking, camping among spruce, fir, and aspen, and scenic driving.

Behind the Rocks Recreation Area, west of Moab, has soaring redrock formations, rock climbing, mountain bike and hiking trails over slickrock, two-wheel- and four-wheel-drive roads, river access, dinosaur tracks, and prehistoric Indian rock art. A popular way to reach it is to drive north of Moab on U.S. 191, then south on Potash Road. The Colorado River Scenic Corridor, accessed from U.S. 128, just north of Moab, has river access, primitive campsites, hiking in side canyons, and mountain biking atop slickrock cliffs. Between U.S. 191 and the Needles is Canyon Rims Recreation Area, a good alternative for dispersed camping and explorations in ranch country.

The multiagency Moab Information Center (MIC) on Main Street is your best bet for more information, maps, books, and other trip planning. It is open daily, 8 a.m. to 9 p.m. in summer; 9 a.m. to 5 p.m. in winter; closed Thanksgiving, Christmas, and New Year's Day; tel. (435) 259-1370.

PAGE 12/13: Curious sandstone formation and the La Sal Mountains seen from near Delicate Arch. PHOTO ©PAUL HIGLEY/LARRY ULRICH STOCK

One of the best overviews of the Arches region can be had from atop the La Sal Mountains, east of the park. From here, it is possible to read the bare land as if it were a 3-D topographical map. Around the edges are the hummocky profiles of volcanoes that never broke the surface: the Henry, Abajo, and La Sal Mountains, and Navajo Mountain. To the west and south, respectively, are the San Rafael Swell, the Waterpocket Fold, and Comb Ridge—monoclines that volcanism has pushed higher on one side than the other, so that they look like frozen waves poised in midair. In between are mesas, buttes, and cliffs and labyrinthian canyons carved by the San Juan, Colorado, and Green Rivers. Their route is marked by lush vegetation, sinuous green lines that stand out against the burnt redrock desert.

Arches National Park is immediately northwest, a friendly huddle of arches, spires, and hoodoos that looks surprisingly orderly from this great height. It is obvious that they have formed along parallel valleys. The orientation coincides with two ancient faults, the northeast-trending Colorado and northwest-trending Olympic-Wichita Lineaments, which intersect in Arches. From above, the formations look like pieces on an enormous game board moved around by an invisible hand.

There IS an invisible presence here: salt. It underlies miles of sedimentary rocks, a relic of an ancient past. Out of sight but always felt, it is salt that has orchestrated this fantasia of stone. Compressed by the sediments covering it, the Paradox salt becomes as free-flowing as table salt, moving away from the

heavy rocks above it, constantly trying to escape the pressure. It finds the perfect outlet along two-billion-year-old Precambrian faults in the rocky basement of Canyon Country, rising to the surface and pushing up overlying strata into salt domes, or diapirs.

The Paradox salt deposits were laid down in a series of intermittent inland seas, beginning 300 million years ago, in the Pennsylvanian geological period. These seas were

trapped in the Paradox Basin, a trough 200 miles long and 100 miles wide bordering the Uncompahgre Uplift, the forerunner to the La Sal Mountains, and several smaller plateaus. While the rest of the western United States lay under a warm, shallow tropical ocean, the Paradox arm in southeastern Utah frequently dried out, leaving behind evaporites made up of anhydrite, salt, and potash. The Paradox Formation can be glimpsed at the bottom of Salt Valley in Arches, where the collapse of the salt anticline and subsequent erosion have exposed the buried formation.

When the climate changed and the sea withdrew to the west, 3,000 feet of Paradox salt was left behind. In time, this salt became

deeply buried under the limestone, shale, and sandstone near-shore deposits of the Pinkerton Trail Formation. That formation, in turn, was covered by layers of red, iron-rich sediments, washed down from the steep sides of the Uncompahgre Uplift, and white dune deposits from the eastern shore of the sea. These red-and-white deposits form the White Rim Sandstone, Organ Rock Shale, Cedar Mesa Sandstone, and Elephant Canyon Formation/Halgaito Shale that together comprise the Cutler Group, beautifully displayed in the banded spires of the Needles District of Canyonlands National Park.

The signature rock of Canyon Country, sandstone, was laid down during the Triassic and Jurassic geological periods, 245 to 144 million years ago, when dinosaurs ruled the land. Early in the Triassic, highlands throughout southern Utah were reduced by erosion to hills whose sediments—clays, silts, sand, and pebbles— filled mountain basins with the soft, crumbly vermilion Moenkopi Formation and banded purple-gray Chinle Formation. The latter contains uranium, which, in the 1950s, lured many miners to Canyonlands in search of big government payoffs.

Sandstone is instantly recognizable by its beautiful reddish hues, uniform texture, and ability to weather into sheer cliffs, alcoves, and arches. During the Jurassic Period, 208 to 144 million years ago, the earth's climate experienced a long, hot drying trend. Much of the West was buffeted by blowing sands, which piled into enormous sand dunes that were crossbedded as the wind changed direction.

ABOVE: The Penguins and Moab Valley. PHOTO ©TOM TILL

The towering orange Wingate Sandstone found in Canyonlands' Island in the Sky District was deposited early in this era. Between the dunes were shallow pools and streams, a favorite haunt of dinosaurs, whose tracks are often seen in the ledgy maroon Kayenta Formation siltstone that settled out in the still water. Several locations in the Moab area, including Arches National Park, preserve dinosaur footprints, making this one of the largest dinosaur trackways in the country. A later period of desertification covered 150,000 square miles of the West with 3,000-foot-high sand dunes.

When the climate changed again and the sea intruded, organic iron and lime cemented the sand grains into the "petrified" dunes of the Navajo Sandstone Formation. The Navajo—a lovely rock formation varying in hue from salmon to tea rose to tan—is the most widespread sandstone in the West, reaching 2,000 feet high in Zion National Park in southwestern Utah. In the Moab area, it can be seen along the Colorado River, atop the Island in the Sky District of Canyonlands National Park. The Navajo underlies the rock spans in Arches National Park. There are larger exposures in the entrance cliffs and the rolling Petrified Dunes near the Windows section.

The formations in Arches are made of a different sandstone, the Entrada, which was laid down in the late Jurassic Period as wind-blown sand dunes and marine deposits. These varied conditions resulted in three different "members"—the brick-red Dewey Bridge, the pink Slick Rock sandstone, and hard white Moab Tongue limestone. Creta-

ceous-era rocks have largely been removed by erosion from Arches but can be seen in Salt Valley and Cache Valley below Delicate Arch, where these layers have collapsed and are exposed. Look for the green-hued Brushy Basin member of the crumbly Morrison Formation, which deposited in a floodplain. Another shale, the brownish Cedar Mountain Formation, lies above the Morrison. It is overlaid by tan-colored Dakota Sandstone, established in a coastal plain, and the yellow-brown Mancos Shale, a marine formation.

Like the Chinle, the Morrison contains the bones of dinosaurs, which became extinct about 65 million years ago, perhaps as a result of a meteor colliding with the earth. Around the same time, a powerful phase of volcanic activity affected the West, apparently linked to movement along the North American and Pacific continental plates off the California coast. Ancient boundary faults extended, squeezed, and twisted the Colorado Plateau. The Rocky Mountains were forced up on the eastern boundary, while the area that is now southeastern Utah folded over itself, creating the dramatic Waterpocket Fold, a monocline

that is higher on one side than the other. In Arches, the Salt Valley Anticline, a warp not unlike a wrinkle in a carpet, rose along the Colorado Fault, and salt pushed up more than a mile of sedimentary rocks, causing them to fracture. On the south side of the park, the Moab Fault runs parallel to U.S. 191 through another collapsed salt valley. An overlook in the entrance cliffs offers graphic evidence of the 2,500-foot fault-block displacement that left Navajo Sandstone rocks, readily seen at the entrance to Arches, barely visible in the cliffs on the other side of the highway.

Another period of volcanic activity, 30 million years ago, in the middle of the Tertiary Period, further compressed faults within the Colorado Plateau and forced it to begin its mile-high rise. The earth movements set in motion the chain of events that led to Canyon Country's unique appearance. The meandering Colorado and Green Rivers, which join in Canyonlands National Park, steepened their gradients and picked up speed, cutting deeply into their winding courses and sculpting labyrinthian canyons. Almost invisible in their canyons, the rivers wrap around horseshoe bends, or entrenched meanders, such as the one below Dead Horse Point State Park. Sediment-laden river water eventually will cut a direct path through bends. When it does, it may create natural bridges, such as those seen at Natural Bridges National Monument, south of Canyonlands, that will eventually become isolated buttes. In Arches, movements along faults caused salt domes to collapse, leaving behind the slumped Cache and Salt Valleys and perfect conditions for the formation of Arches.

HOW ARCHES FORM

Skyline Arch, late afternoon.

The more than 2,000 known arches and other openings in Arches National Park are made from eroded Entrada Sandstone. They are the result of a long process of weathering that began when the salt domes in Salt and Cache Valleys collapsed 30 million years ago, and young Cretaceous rocks were removed by weathering, revealing the Entrada Sandstone below. Once exposed, the Entrada expanded and cracked, leaving linear joints beside these valleys that are vulnerable to erosion. Groundwater entering the joints dissolves the salt. Freeze-thaw cycles, common at this mile-high elevation, wedge open the cracks until high-walled corridors separated by thin sandstone walls, or fins, appear.

Fins are the first stage in the formation of arches. Persistent erosion attacks small recesses in the rock. As water washes out the calcite and iron cementing the rock, grains of sand are re-moved and form sand dunes beneath the rocks. As the recess enlarges, it spalls like a peeling onion and an alcove forms. With luck, some alcoves will open into windows and eventually becomes arches.

Alcoves and arches are often found in the uni-form Navajo Sandstone, the rock immediately be-low the Entrada. But the Entrada's three mem-bers—the Dewey Bridge, the Slick Rock, and Moab Tongue Formations—offer perfect arch-forming characteristics, with the two lower formations eas-ily sculpted by erosion and the hard, marine-formed Moab Tongue an effective caprock protect-ing the formation.

Not all arches form in fins. Some begin in caves and are gouged out by weathering. Still others start life as water-filled potholes on the edge of a cliff. Over time, the water breaks through the base of the pool and leaves behind a pothole arch—a cross between a natural arch and a natural bridge.

When it comes, transformation is often swift. Before 1940, Skyline Arch was called Arch-in-the-Making, but a rockfall enlarged the window over-night and a fully fledged young arch was born. On the other end of the spectrum is 306-foot-long, 11-foot-wide Landscape Arch in Devils Garden, one of the longest known arches in the world. Landscape is a mature arch, characterized by a delicate, slender appearance. A large chunk of the arch fell down in 1991 and smaller pieces fell in the following few years. It is only a matter of time before the whole arch falls, leaving behind two isolated columns exposed to the elements. Differ-ential erosion—weathering of rock layers of dif-ferent types and hardnesses—sculpts the strange pillars, or hoodoos, that crop up throughout the park. Perhaps the most famous is much-photo-graphed Balance Rock in the Windows section.

OPPOSITE: Landscape Arch, winter morning in Devils Garden. PHOTO ©GLENN VAN NIMWEGEN

The Human Landscape

La Sal Mountains and bizarre formations near The Windows. PHOTO ©BRUCE HUCKO

Every pilgrimage in the desert is a pilgrimage to self.
There is no place to hide, and so we are found.
—Terry Tempest Williams
Red: Passion and Patience in the Desert

In December 1922, Hungarian miner Alexander Ringhoffer was prospecting in the Klondike Bluffs, in the remote northwestern section of Arches, when he chanced upon beautiful Minaret Arch and left an inscription there. Like many miners who realized that there was more gold in tourists' pockets than in the ground, Ringhoffer was convinced that the area he dubbed Devils Garden had tourism potential. The following summer, he guided exectives of the Denver and Rio Grande Railroad to the site, who in turn lobbied Congress to make the area a national monument.

Ironically, six years later, when Arches National Monument was set aside, the area now called Klondike Bluffs was left out and, through a survey error, the name Devils Garden was conferred on the area that contains Landcape Arch. The Klondike Bluffs were part of a 53-square-mile addition to the national monument on November 25, 1938. Minaret Arch is now called Tower Arch and is considered the founding arch of the park.

It is early September when I drive the dirt road through Salt Valley to Klondike Bluffs. I bump along for nine miles through empty country charged with stillness. Near the Bluffs, I pass the Marching Men, a series of fantastically eroded spires in the southern cliffs. They do, indeed, seem like sentries guarding the treasures within.

I park in the deserted parking lot and begin climbing the cliffs. At the top I have a panoramic view of Arches and the country beyond. On the east are Skyline Arch, the distant Windows, Dry Mesa, and the La Sal Mountains. To the north is Devils Garden. The southern horizon is filled with the long wall of red sandstone that parallels the Moab Fault along U.S. 191. The silence is so profound my ears start ringing.

Studies in Canyonlands have recorded an acoustic level one notch above that found in a soundproof recording studio. Ambient sound levels and crowds in national parks have increased to such a degree that the National Park Service now manages silence and solitude as a resource. Canyon Country's silence is truly rare, one of its greatest resources. Caught up in the busy-ness of civilization, perhaps we don't notice noise pollution anymore or the effect that our expanding global population has on our nerves. Airplanes buzz across the Grand Canyon. Idling vehicles sit at overlooks. Larger numbers of hikers on popular trails means more talk and socializing. Campgrounds have the look, as my friend Jeff commented, of refugee camps, which perhaps they are, as we increasingly flee our stressful urban lives.

Even the shortest hikes outdoors can strip away the armor of culture and lay us bare to ourselves. We begin to speak in the language of the heart, not the mind. There is a fellowship in nature that is lacking in our man-made environments, which, for all our ingenuity, are limited by a human view of the world. For me, true diversity embraces other life forms as well as different cultures and requires a reciprocity we still seem unable to envision. I doubt that nature minds, but I sense that it is we who are diminished.

A small hawk flies directly in front of me, oblivious to my presence. A cottontail bolts from behind a rock and disappears into a clump of dark-gray skeletal blackbrush. Stink beetles crawl slowly across sand, then disappear into holes in the ground. There is a rustling in a stately old juniper, the ear-splitting squawk of a jay, then silence. To the northwest are jointed cliffs that have been weathered into odd fins. They are tilted at almost a 45-degree angle. I marvel that they can stay upright at all. Like so many other features in the park, the redrocks seem choreographed to geological perfection, graceful, soaring, bending, leaping. Everything seems to be in motion, sliding out of view in a long slow freefall.

I cross a wash of sun-baked mud strewn with debris from a recent flashflood and begin the steep climb up a huge sand dune, pacing myself in the mounting heat. At the top I stop and guzzle water. Ahead of me is a wide corridor, which funnels a pleasant breeze. I can see where a coyote has passed through; its doggy prints are pressed firmly into moist sand. Nearby are heart-shaped

Profuse display of sunflowers in Salt Valley.

mule deer tracks.

The last time I hiked here I saw mountain lion tracks. There are none today, but I scan the ledges above, anyway. The thought of meeting a mountain lion is thrilling and terrifying at the same time. I live with cats and love their fierce beauty, intelligence, and self-possession. But they are also cruel and opportunistic hunters. I am not mistress here, I am potential prey. I start whistling loudly to announce my presence and walk a little faster.

A little farther and Tower Arch appears suddenly on my right. It blends so well with the cliffs I don't see it until I am right below. Nearby, a tall hoodoo pillar protected by the hard white Moab Tongue member of the Entrada Sandstone stands erect, enclosed in the circle of stone. It looks like a giant pagan fertility pole erupting from a gash in the earth. Clambering up the smooth slickrock, I rest in the arch's precious shade, eat lunch, then take a nap. I dream I am being led across the desert by a mountain lion who is teaching me animal stories about every rock we pass. The journey we take together seems important—preparation for a role I don't yet understand. I awake filled with a nameless longing.

Tower Arch, Klondike Bluffs area.

North

Collared Lizard

ARCHES

KLONDIKE BLUFFS

DEVILS GARDEN

LANDSCAPE ARCH ✦

✦ DEVILS GARDEN TRAILHEAD

SALT

SKYLINE ARCH ✦

VALLEY

NATIONAL

✦ SAND DUNE ARCH

FIERY FURNACE

FIERY FURNACE VIEW

DELICATE ARCH

SALT VALLEY OVERLOOK

WOLFE RANCH ✦

DELICATE ARCH VIEWPOINT

PANORAMA POINT

BALANCED ROCK ✦

ROCK PINNACLES

GARDEN OF EDEN

THE WINDOWS

✦ DOUBLE ARCH

✦ NORTH & SOUTH WINDOWS

TURRET ARCH ✦

THE GREAT WALL

Courthouse

✦ PETRIFIED DUNES VIEW

PETRIFIED DUNES

Wash

PARK

SHEEP ROCK ✦

✦ TOWER OF BABEL

THREE GOSSIPS ✦

✦ COURTHOUSE TOWERS VIEW

COURTHOUSE TOWERS

✦ THE ORGAN

PARK AVENUE TRAILHEAD ✦

LA SAL MOUNTAINS VIEW

Colorado River

VISITOR CENTER

TO CRESCENT JUNCTION

191

TO CANYONLANDS AND DEAD HORSE POINT

313

TO CASTLE VALLEY

128

128

❖ MOAB

279

KANE CREEK ROAD

191

TO POTASH

TO MONTICELLO

ILLUSTRATION BY DARLECE CLEVELAND

Arches National Park is located in southeastern Utah, fives miles north of Moab, the closest town for lodging, food, gas, and other visitor services. The park preserves more than 2,000 known natural arches, windows, and other red sandstone formations. It was set aside as a 4,520-acre national monument on April 12, 1929. It was upgraded to a national park in 1971, and with the addition of 3,140-acre Lost Spring Canyon in 1998, now covers, by official estimate, 76,358.95 acres, or roughly 120 square miles.

Most park features can be seen by driving the paved scenic road and hiking short trails. Landscape Arch and other arches can be viewed from a moderate to difficult 7.2-mile scenic trail loop in Devils Garden. Delicate Arch is visible from a moderately strenuous 3-mile round-trip trail or two easy overlooks in Salt Valley. Ranger-led hikes into the Fiery Furnace are offered daily, between April and October, for a fee. Sign up early for these popular hikes at the visitor center. Stay on trails to avoid crushing cryptobiotic soil, the dark soil crust essential to desert plant life.

Arches has an elevation of 3,960 to 5,653 feet and is very exposed. Temperatures reach 110 degrees in summer and single digits in winter. Come with appropriate clothing. In summer, cover bare skin and use a high SPF-factor sunscreen, wear a broad-brimmed hat and sunglasses, and carry and drink a liter of water on short trails; a gallon or more on long hikes. The campground has 52 tent and trailer sites, available on a first-come, first-served basis; register at the entrance station or visitor center. Flush toilets and water are available. Two walk-in group sites for tent campers may be reserved for 11 or more people. Contact Southeastern Utah Group, National Park Service, 2282 S. West Resource Boulevard, Moab, UT 84532-8000 or fax (435) 259-4285.

The visitor center is located near the entrance station and has park information, ranger talks, an audiovisual program, books, maps, exhibits, restrooms, and drinking water. It is open 8 a.m. to 4:30 p.m. daily, with extended hours seasonally. For more information, contact: Superintendent, Arches National Park, P.O. Box 907, Moab, UT 84532-0907; (435) 719-2299 or www.nps.gov/arch. Information is also available at the multiagency Moab Information Center (MIC) on Center Street and Main. Hours are 8 a.m. to 9 p.m. in summer; 9 a.m. to 5 p.m. in winter; tel. (435) 259-1370; closed Thanksgiving, Christmas, and New Year's Day.

HUMAN HISTORY

The first people in the Southwest were paleoindians whose ancestors had crossed the Bering Strait during the last ice age, when Asia and the Americas were joined by a land bridge. Spreading south, these paleoindians pursued woolly mastodons, camels, giant bison, and ground sloths across the savannah grasslands that then existed on the Colorado Plateau. The hunters moved with the big game herds, slept in cave shelters, flaked stone tools around campfires, and butchered onsite, leaving behind occasional bones, chipped stone, and beautiful chert spear points of a type known as Clovis and Folsom, for the towns in New Mexico where they were first found. Although no physical evidence of paleoindians has been found within Arches, we know these hunters were in the area because Folsom projectile points have been found nearby.

As the climate warmed, the big-game herds died out. Humans, however, adapted. By 6,000 B.C., they had become nomadic hunter-gatherers who moved seasonally across the Southwest. They hunted bighorn sheep, rabbits, and other small game using a spear thrower known as an *atlatl* and harvested seed-bearing grasses, nuts, fruits, and other wild foods. By fitting themselves into the changing environment, Archaic people thrived in southeastern Utah for millennia.

There are indications that late in Archaic time, things began to go awry, perhaps due to a persistent drought that disrupted food sources. Hunters began secreting split-twig hunting fetishes of game animals next to high ledges, probably to ensure a good hunt. Life-size images of limbless, hollow-eyed, E.T.-like beings were painted on sandstone walls deep in remote Colorado River canyons, such as Barrier Canyon (now known as Horseshoe Canyon) in Canyonlands. Haunting Barrier Canyon-style rock can also be seen in Arches National Park. The Moab Panel, as it is called, may be viewed from a trail above Courthouse Wash, next to U.S. 191. It was badly vandalized in 1980 and 1986 and has been partially restored.

The soaring redrock cliffs along the Colorado River also preserve rock art by the later Ancestral Pueblo and Fremont cultures. These cultures were probably an outgrowth of the Archaic but were influenced by new lifeways that originated in Mexico, where agriculture, pottery, and building with stone had already been invented. By A.D. 500, extended family groups were growing corn beside water sources and hunting bighorn sheep, deer, rabbits, and other game using bows and arrows. They wove beautifully intricate baskets for gathering and storing plants. Home was a cool semicircular pithouse built into the ground, propped up by large wooden supports, and roofed with criss-crossed beams, latticework, and earth.

Agriculture required planning and cooperation, but also allowed villagers more free time for creative expression. By A.D. 1000, both Fremont and Ancestral Puebloans had developed distinctive pottery styles, using local clay, individual patterns, and different firing methods. Although Fremont people still preferred pithouses, Ancestral Puebloans now built mud-plastered stone buildings that could be expanded—story by story, room by room—for housing and storage. Pueblos were built around a central plaza, which provided more room for daily activities. Underground ceremonial rooms, or *kivas*, were a spiritual connection to pithouse living, used by clans and communities for rituals based on the seasonal agricultural calendar. Southeastern Utah's rugged topography slowed settlement, but by the 1200s, even remote canyons had attracted settlers who built small, hidden homes and granaries in high alcoves along tributaries of the Colorado and Green Rivers.

Ancestral Pueblo people had moved south to New Mexico and Arizona by A.D. 1300, probably due to a long drought, diminishing natural resources, and increased tensions among villages that sparked violence and ritual killings across the Four Corners. Little is known of the Fremont. They may have become culturally indistinct from Pueblo people or joined incoming Paiutes, a branch of Utes living by water.

By the time Spanish explorer Juan Maria Antonio Rivera arrived in the Moab area in 1765, Numic-speaking Utes from Southern California were established in the Arches area

ABOVE: The Barrier Canyon Style pictographs of the Moab Panel. PHOTO ©TOM TILL

and following a hunting and gathering lifestyle, using horses acquired from Spanish settlers. Their neighbors to the south were the Navajo, Athabascans from northwest Canada who split into Apache and Navajo on arrival in the Southwest. A panel displaying Ute petroglyphs can be seen on the Delicate Arch Trail.

The Colorado River, which runs for 11 miles along the park's southern boundary, was shallow enough to ford here and attracted Spanish, Mexican, then American travelers. Spaniards merely passed through, trading with Utes and Navajos, on their way to Santa Fe. The route that would eventually be called the Old Spanish Trail, linking Los Angeles and Santa Fe, was actually blazed by Americans William Wolfskill and George C. Yount in 1830-31 under Mexican rule. In 1844, just before Mexico ceded most of the Southwest to the United States, Denis Julien, a French-Canadian trapper, came down the Colorado River and carved his name in Canyonlands and in Devils Garden in Arches.

In 1855, members of the Mormon Elk Mountain Mission built a fort in the lower Moab Valley but were quickly driven out by Utes. It wasn't until after the Civil War, when American ranchers, miners, and other settlers began to flood into the West, that Moab was founded. Among the better-known homesteaders was African-American William Granstaff, who ran a ranch near the Colorado in 1881. Granstaff was forced to leave after he was accused of selling liquor to the Utes. The canyon he lived in is remembered today as Negro Bill Canyon. Moab suddenly

boomed in the 1950s, when uranium was found nearby, then bust as the government market disappeared. Today, it is booming again, as a center of outdoor recreation.

The first (and only) white settlers in Arches were John Wesley Wolfe and his son Fred. In 1898, they built a small ranch near the junction of Salt Wash and Winter Camp Wash, just west of Delicate Arch, and managed to make a go of it for 12 years. John Wesley Wolfe was a Civil War veteran from Tennessee who was crippled in the Siege of Vicksburg in 1863. Married twice, with four children, Wolfe seems to have suffered from wanderlust and preferred a solitary life away from civilization. He and Fred were later joined by Fred's sister Flora and her husband Ed Stanley. Flora and her family are pictured in the oldest known photograph of Delicate Arch. The Wolfe Cabin (sometimes called the Turnbow Cabin for a later owner) has been restored and may be viewed at the Delicate Arch trailhead.

Hungarian miner and prospector Alexander Ringhoffer succeeded in getting Arches set aside as a national monument in 1929; two other local men helped expand it.

John W. "Doc" Williams, Moab's first permanent physician, arrived in the frontier town in 1897 and lived there until his death in 1956, at the age of 103. Williams took every opportunity to drive visitors to the area in one of the automobiles from a dealership he ran on the side. Doc Williams Point, a promontory west of the Fiery Furnace, commemorates this longtime booster. Loren "Bish" Taylor, editor of Moab's newspaper, *The Times-Independent*, was born into one of the founding families of Moab. He used the bully pulpit of the paper and his political capital in the community to successfully lobby Franklin D. Roosevelt about expanding the park in 1938.

Arches was named by Southwestern National Monuments superintendent Frank Pinkley in 1925. Eight years later, an NPS-sponsored scientific expedition named many of the famous arches. The first onsite superintendent of Arches was Russell Mahan, who arrived as custodian in 1944 and was appointed superintendent in 1948. He was succeeded by Bates Wilson, who served as superintendent of Arches from 1949 to 1972. Raised on a cattle ranch in New Mexico, Bates Wilson was the quintessential independent-minded "desert rat," who was happiest Jeeping around his domain, cooking for guests, and working to get adjoining Canyonlands set aside as a new national park.

VISITING THE PARK

Tadpole shrimp in an ephemeral pothole.   PHOTO ©GLENN VAN NIMWEGEN

*The desert is a good place—clean,
honest, dangerous, uncluttered, strong,
open, big, vibrant with legend.*
——Edward Abbey
Confessions of a Barbarian

Morning sun is hitting the 1,000-foot-high Navajo Sandstone cliffs above the Colorado River as we pull our two canoes ashore at the southern boundary of Arches National Park. Exchanging river shoes for hiking boots, we lather on sunscreen, soak bandannas, don hats, and check water bottles. At 8:30 a.m, the temperature is already soaring. Gone are the cool, rainy conditions of the last few days. We're in for a scorcher.

The rain is the reason we are here this morning. I am hiking into the Arches backcountry with Tim Graham, an ecologist for the Biological Resources Discipline of the U.S. Geological Survey. Tim's specialty is the uniquely adapted microfauna in desert potholes, the depressions in rock that fill with water when it rains. It was Harvard biologist E. O. Wilson who coined the term *biophilia*, "the connections that human beings subconsciously seek with the rest of life." Tim, I note, is a biophile, passionate about living things. His enthusiasm is infectious. I am really looking forward to today.

Since it's the Labor Day holiday, Tim has brought along his wife Audrey, a former ranger at Arches, their 12-year-old daughter Tessie, and his research assistant, Wyatt. We hike toward the cliffs and begin friction-climbing the steep slickrock, inching around narrow ledges, and resting in alcoves. We pace ourselves in the heat, drinking water and creating "evaporative cooling" by spraying exposed skin with a water bottle. Life is so stripped down here, it seems remarkable when we come upon a bright-orange velvet ant on the redrock. This little wingless wasp squeaks to scare us away and disappears into blackbrush.

Behind us are breathtaking views of the Colorado River and the Slickrock Bike Trail in the opposite cliffs. Higher up, we can see the Windows Section of Arches in the distance. To the east is Dry

Mesa and Dome Plateau, a 35,000-acre roadless area that was part of Arches National Monument but was left out when it became a national park. The Arches backcountry is wilder than the developed part of the park leads you to expect; it is composed of cliffs, canyons, and dry washes with no trails or shelter. Overnight hikers may only enter it by NPS permit. I'm glad to be with people familiar with the terrain. This is no place to hike alone.

Tim first started monitoring here 12 years ago and has mapped a route. Following the line of cliffs, he shows us "Elephant's Graveyard," a series of oddly eroded rocks that look like elephant feet, and three large cliffside potholes, or *tinajas*, filled with water. Hopping between two pools are tiny red-spotted and spadefoot toads, which stay moist as water evaporates from potholes by digging themselves into the mud with shiny black projections on their hind feet called spades and covering themselves with mucus.

We follow the crossbedding in the ancient dune-formed sandstone up to the cliff tops and locate the first of the 53 potholes in Tim's study sample. About half have water and are buzzing with life. Tim notes the size of the pools, the amount of sediment in them, water depth and temperature, and uses a Global Positioning System (GPS) device to record precise geographic coordinates. He takes out a little dipper that looks like a butterfly net, scoops the water, and extracts fairy shrimp, tadpole shrimp, and clam shrimp, gnats, backswimmers, snails, and beetles. A wasp is floating on the surface of one pothole. Its wings are fanned out to dry, creating a daisy pattern on the bottom of the shallow pool. From below, it looks like a predatory dragonfly. The shrimp swim away in a hurry.

These fairy shrimp are what intrigue Tim the most. Their eggs are *cryptobiotic* (life-suspending), which means they can lose more than 90 percent of their water content and still remain viable. The fairy shrimp do this, apparently, by using sugars such as trehalose to preserve the complicated molecular structure of proteins and lipids that retains cellular memory as the tissues dehydrate. This extraordinary process allows the shrimp to survive remarkable odds. Eggs have been exposed to the ionizing radiation and

Lower Courthouse Wash near its confluence with the Colorado River.

vacuum of outer space, then hatched back on earth. Medicine has already come up with ways of using cryptobiosis to stabilize antibiotics. But Tim is far less pragmatic. "I just think they are really neat," he says, grinning, as he crouches over a pool.

Dehydration, which allows the shrimp to survive, is deadly to humans. I am about to learn just how deadly. After six hours in 100-degree-plus temperatures and very little shade, I have reached my heat tolerance. No matter how much water I drink or spray on me, I remain hot, red-faced, and unable to perspire, my core body temperature rising dangerously. I stay calm by precisely monitoring what is happening inside my body: overheated brain, fuzziness, muscle weakness, shaking, headache, nausea, confusion, and stumbling. Trained as an Emergency Medical Technician, Audrey tells me that fair Europeans sometimes go straight from overheating to heatstroke and bypass heat exhaustion. Tim assures me that this is genetic and even my years of acclimation in the

Southwest may not override it. They remain upbeat and encouraging, sticking close and offering me the last of their water. Tess keeps me talking, debating the merits of Harry Potter versus Lord of the Rings. Wyatt carries my backpack. Audrey keeps soaking me down. I know I am in good hands and relax.

We reach the Colorado River safely and cool off by swimming back to our cars, while Tim follows, paddling one canoe and pulling the other. We end the day over a homecooked meal at the Graham house, sanctuary for Tim's research technicians, as well as a motley assortment of dogs, toads, kids, and foster babies. I am touched by their easy-going generosity toward a stranger. I found what my yoga teacher calls my "edge" today and am fortunate that it was with such supportive, experienced companions. Many are not so lucky. Each year, people die in the Arches area from dehydration. The sun can kill. Carry water and respect your limits.

Cryptobiotic soil in slickrock "pavement".

PHOTO ©JEFF D. NICHOLAS

Cryptobiotic crust, the dark biological soil crust that covers more than 70 percent of the Colorado Plateau, is one of the quiet miracles of Canyon Country. For years, no one gave this odd, crumbly ground covering much thought. All that changed when Jayne Belnap, a biologist at the U.S. Geological Service's Forest and Rangeland Ecosystem Science Center in Moab, decided to take a closer look. What Belnap unearthed was a remarkable story of biological adaptation, dating back to the dawn of life on earth.

Cryptobiotic soil (the term *cryptobiotic* means "hidden life" in Greek) is actually a community of mutually beneficial living organisms, which work together to reduce erosion, increase water retention, and encourage soil fertility. On the Colorado Plateau, cryptobiotic crust communities are dominated by cyanobacteria (blue-green algae), one of the oldest life forms on earth, as well as

lichens, mosses, microfungi, bacteria, and green algae. Cyanobacteria and microfungi protect themselves from sharp sand grains by secreting a sticky mucilage around their cells that helps glue soil particles in place. They also contribute nitrogen to soil. Mosses and lichens put down small roots that anchor the soil and keep it from blowing away.

When it rains, these organisms and their mucilage absorb up to 10 times their volume in water and then release it slowly into the soil once the rain ends. High-desert frost-heaving, the principal agent in forming the geological landmarks at Arches, also works to roughen the surface of cryptobiotic soil, further slowing rainwater runoff and increasing water infiltration into the soil. Mature cryptobiotic crusts are easy to recognize: the soil is dark, mounded, crumbly, and filled with plants. Less easy to see are young soil crusts, which look like matted sandy soil.

Hiking, camping, bicycling, and off-road driving are destroying cryptobiotic crusts faster than they can be restored. Crushed crusts contribute less nitrogen and organic matter to the ecosystem, dry out, and blow away, forming sand dunes that bury other healthy crusts. Native grasses and other plants are then replaced by woody plants like pinyons, junipers, and sagebrush, cutting down on biodiversity in the desert. Recovery can take up to 250 years. Bicycle and tire tracks are particularly damaging because they form a continuous strip and channelize water flow that quickly washes away soil. To preserve biological soil crusts, keep to established roads and trails. Where there is no trail, travel on slickrock or in washes. Camp in designated sites, on slickrock, under trees, or on sandy beaches. Remember: Don't bust the crust. For more information, log on to www.soilcrust.org.

POTHOLES

Potholes near La Sal Mountains Viewpoint.

Potholes are eroded basins found in sandstone cliffs across the Colorado Plateau. Large potholes are called *tanks* or *tinajas* in Spanish. Pothole specialist Tim Graham reserves the term *"tinaja"* for basins in drainages primarily carved by water; depressions away from drainages, principally excavated by wind, he dubs "potholes." The waterpockets in Capitol Reef are, therefore, *tinajas*, whereas those atop cliffs in Arches and Canyonlands are true potholes. When it rains, potholes fill with water and the cementing minerals between grains of sand dissolve, allowing the sediments to be removed by wind when the pothole dries out.

Thousands of tiny plants and animals have evolved ways of living in these temporary aquatic habitats. Only single-celled organisms survive in small, shallow pools. Slightly larger potholes may contain tardigrades (water bears), rotifers, nematodes, and water mites. Larger potholes might also support thousands of gnat larvae. The largest pools contain the most diversity: fairy shrimp, clam shrimp, tadpole shrimp, water fleas, and other small crustaceans; snails; and mosquito larvae, diving beetles, backswimmers, water boatmen, and other insects.

On the Colorado Plateau most rain arrives in April, August, and October but is unpredictable at best. Pothole species have, therefore, evolved strategies that allow them to wait indefinitely for pools to fill, then quickly revive, reproduce, and complete their life cycles before water evaporates. Water temperature, pool depth, salinity, and rate of evaporation are all important factors in who lives and who dies in this unique environment.

Thousands of creatures, representing up to a dozen species, coexist in a single pothole. Those that can survive dehydration, extreme heat and cold, solar radiation, and salinity by shutting down metabolic activity and entering a dormant state known as *cryptobiosis* are the most successful. Once rehydrated, though, they must complete their life cycles fast or die. Some fairy shrimp, for example, complete their life cycles in less than four days. Gnat eggs and larvae are also cryptobiotic, but rotifers, tardigrades, and nematodes can dry up and survive at any time in their life cycle. Snails employ what Tim Graham dubs "the Tupperware strategy": a water-tight shell that seals water inside for a few months while they lie buried in sediments

Spadefoot and red-spotted toads begin mating as soon as pools fill and lay eggs that can hatch within 24 hours, metamorphosing from tadpoles to toads in two or three weeks. Once the toads have legs they survive the evaporation of the pothole by hopping away to places with deeper soils, such as cracks in rock. There the toadlets dig down to moister sediments and hide, staying hydrated by covering themselves with mucus. Winged insects, such as beetles, mosquitoes, and gnats, are the best adapted escape artists; they simply fly away.

Pothole life is fragile and easily disturbed. Never wade or splash in a pothole, drink from it, or even walk, ride, or drive through a dry pothole, if you can avoid it.

OPPOSITE: Potholes in lower Park Avenue. PHOTO ©TOM TILL

Sun bursting through a small arch in the tail of Sheep Rock, Courthouse Towers.   PHOTO ©BRUCE HUCKO

Park Avenue is the first major attraction on the 18-mile paved scenic road through the park. It is a narrow canyon with high sandstone walls made up of the Dewey Bridge and overlying Slick Rock members of Entrada Sandstone. Early travelers thought it looked like New York's Park Avenue, a busy city street with tall buildings. On the western wall are two balanced rocks: Queen Nefertiti and Sausage Rock. Queen Nefertiti is named for its striking resemblance to the famous 14th-century bust of the Egyptian queen. Across the canyon is an eroded wall thought to resemble another queen: Britain's Queen Victoria. A mile-long, one-way trail leads from the Park Avenue parking lot to the Courthouse Towers parking lot. Either have a car meet you or return to the Park Avenue parking lot.

Beyond Park Avenue is Courthouse Towers, which contains tall sandstone landmarks reminis-cent of those in Monument Valley, Arizona. Some of the famous rocks here are Baby Arch, Sheep Rock, Tower of Babel, and the Three Gossips. Baby Arch (formerly known as Hole-in-the-Wall) is a small arch between Sheep Rock and a tall fin to the south, which geologists conjecture may have once been two large arches that fell. These monolithic rocks were formed by erosion of a collapsed anticline after Courthouse Wash and its tributaries exposed underlying sandstone.

Running north from Courthouse Towers to near Balanced Rock, west of the scenic road, is the Great Wall, a prominent sandstone cliff containing arches, spires, and hoodoos—many of which are unmarked on maps and unsigned. Bean Pot Arch was once called Schmidt Arch for its discoverer, Henry G. Schmidt, custodian of Arches from 1939 to 1942. The Lovers is about a mile northeast of Courthouse Wash bridge. Continuing the theme is the Phallus—one of many erotic rocks in Canyon Country—about 3 miles from the bridge. The Poodle, a strangely ruffed rock, is 5 miles from the bridge.

Park Avenue and Courthouse Towers have served as scenic backdrops to a number of Hollywood movies. *Ten Who Dared*, a 1959 film about Major John Wesley Powell's expedition down the Colorado River, *Cheyenne Autumn*, a 1963 movie starring Richard Widmark and directed by John Ford, and *Indiana Jones and the Last Crusade*, directed by Steven Spielberg in 1988, were partly shot in Park Avenue. Courthouse Towers is clearly recognizable in the 1990 movie *Thelma and Louise* as the location where Susan Sarandon and Geena Davis disarm a police officer and lock him in the trunk of his patrol car.

OPPOSITE: Utah juniper and Queen Nefertiti, Park Avenue. PHOTO ©JACK DYKINGA **PAGE 36/37:** Courthouse Towers seen from Park Avenue, late afternoon. PHOTO ©CAROL POLICH

The Windows Section and the La Sal Mountains, sunset.   PHOTO ©RANDALL K. ROBERTS

East of the Great Wall are the Petrified Dunes, the largest outcropping of 200-million-year-old Navajo Sandstone in the park. The beige to pink Navajo underlies the red Entrada Sandstone and, like the Slick Rock member of that formation, was formed as sand dunes in desert conditions. It is exposed as cliffs on the east side of the Moab Fault, paralleling U.S. 191, north of Moab, and along the Colorado River Corridor, scenic Utah 123, running east of Moab.

About 9 miles from the visitor center are some of Arches' most famous landmarks: Balanced Rock and the Windows. Balanced Rock is 128 feet tall and is a classic hoodoo, formed by differential erosion. The Dewey Bridge member of the Entrada Sandstone makes up the base and the harder, over-lying Slickrock member forms the boulder. Author Edward Abbey lived in a trailer near Balanced Rock while working in Arches as a seasonal ranger in the 1950s and 1960s. Chip-off-the-old-Block, a small spire next to Balanced Rock, toppled during the winter of 1975-76. Balanced Rock will one day do the same.

A 3-mile paved loop road turns east past Balanced Rock and winds past Ham Rock, the Garden of Eden, Cove Arch, and Parade of Elephants to a parking lot. A spur road leads to the Garden of Eden, which contains a large group of hoodoo rocks, including Adam and Eve, Devil's Golf Ball, and Owl Rock. The latter was formerly known as Eagle Rock. It was renamed when the rock fell in March 1941.

Park at the parking lot and hike an easy 1-mile loop to Turret Arch and North and South Windows, also called the Spectacles. North Window is the smaller of the openings, with a span of 93 feet and a height of 51 feet. South Window is 105 feet long and 66 feet high. Beyond the South Window, a primitive trail continues around the formation. It is somewhat more strenuous than the first section. Turret Arch is located along the same trail. It has two openings, the largest of which is 64 feet high with a 39-foot span. Be sure to climb up and enjoy the views of the La Sal Mountains. A 400-yard-long trail, leaving from the north section of the parking lot, leads to Double Arch. The larger opening here is 163 feet long and 105 feet high; the smaller has a 60-foot span and a height of 61 feet.

OPPOSITE: Balanced Rock and rising Moon. PHOTO ©JEFF GNASS

Delicate Arch, sunset.

From the Windows Section, the scenic road passes Panorama Point and begins to drop down into Salt Valley, a jumble of collapsed Cretaceous rocks slumped next to sandstone fins. A 2.2-mile paved spur road turns right at Cache Valley and leads to the Delicate Arch area.

Just over a mile from the turnoff is the parking lot for Delicate Arch Trail, a 3-mile round-trip hike over slickrock to the famous landmark. Carry a liter of water per person; this trail is very hot and exposed and gains 480 feet in elevation. It is best at sunset. At the base of the trail is the restored 1906 Wolfe Cabin and corrals, the second ranch built by Civil War veteran John Wesley Wolfe and his family, residents here from 1898 to 1910. Just past the cabin is a rock art panel displaying many Ute petroglyphs.

By park standards, Delicate Arch is small—just 33 feet wide and 45 feet high. It is its unique shape and dramatic setting that draws photographers from around the world. Perched on the edge of Cache Valley with the La Sal Mountains in the distance, the arch seemed delicate to the 1933-34 scientific expedition that named it. Weathering has continued to whittle the Slick Rock member of the Entrada Sandstone that makes up the bulk of the arch beneath its 5-foot protective cap of Moab Tongue member rock. Some people think the arch looks like a pair of bow-legged cowboy chaps or old-lady's bloomers. What do you think? Drive a mile past the main trailhead and you'll find two easier trails that offer more distant views of Delicate Arch. One trail goes up to a low ridge to a viewpoint. A 100-yard trail leads to a wheelchair-accessible viewpoint.

Continuing north, the main park road climbs out of Salt Valley to the Fiery Furnace parking lot. Popular ranger-led hikes into this maze of fiery red sandstone fins and formations are offered daily, otherwise entry is by permit only. Inquire at the visitor center. Of the 18 known arches here, the most dramatic arch may well be Skull Arch, or Twin Arch, which has two openings that look like empty eye sockets in a cranium. Surprise Arch, a larger span at 63 feet long and 55 feet high, was named by former superintendent Bates Wilson in December 1963 while he was trailblazing in the Fiery Furnace. Bates was carefully walking through deeply jointed rocks when he looked up and suddenly saw the arch, hence the name. In the eastern part of the Fiery Furnace is Cliff Arch, or Abbey's Arch, discovered by famed writer Edward Abbey who was a seasonal ranger here in the 1950s when he found it.

OPPOSITE: Fins of the Fiery Furnace and the La Sal Mountains. PHOTO ©TOM TILL

Skyline Arch, early morning light.

PHOTO ©LAURENCE PARENT

About 17 miles north of the visitor center is Sand Dune Arch, in the northern section of Fiery Furnace, an easy hike for youngsters who can then roll around in the sand below the arch. From here, a 1.3-mile roundtrip trail leads over open grasslands to Broken Arch and a back way into Devils Garden campground beyond. Of particular interest on the next mile of the park road is elegant Skyline Arch, which is now 69 feet and 45 feet high. Skyline was officially born in November 1940, when a major rockfall doubled the size of what was then called Arch-in-the-Making.

Broken Arch and Skyline are in the southern section of Devils Garden, which preserves 64 arches along the northeastern rim of Salt Valley. Devils Garden and the Windows formed the nucleus of the original Arches National Monument when it was set aside in 1929. There is a large

parking lot for the main trailhead, with toilets and water available all year. A long loop trail leads through the wide sandy spaces between fins past a number of spectacular arches; primitive spur trails lead to others.

The focal point of any hike here is a visit to Landscape Arch, 0.8-mile from the trailhead. Landscape is second only to Kolob Arch in Zion National Park for title of longest known arch and is 306 feet long, 106 feet high, 11 feet wide at its narrowest part, and 6 feet thick at its thinnest point. It was named by Frank Beckwith, leader of the 1934 Arches National Monument Scientific Expedition. While Skyline is an immature arch, Landscape is a perfect example of a mature arch, destined to fall in the not too distant future. A large rockfall made it even more slender in 1991. No climbing is allowed on the arch.

Just beyond Landscape are Partition, Wall, and Navajo Arches, the latter named by park superintendent Bates Wilson for a Navajo worker who found it. From here on, the trail gets more difficult, with rocky footing, elevation changes, narrow passageways, and some exposure to heights. For those looking for a little solitude and adventure, though, the hike to trail's end is worth it for views of Double O Arch and a prominent spire called Dark Angel. Hikers can return to Landscape Arch from Double O Arch via a 2.2-mile primitive loop or, equipped with a topo map and plenty of water, explore some of the interesting canyons beyond. Note: backcountry permits, available at the visitor center, are required for all overnight trips.

OPPOSITE: Pine Tree Arch, Devils Garden. PHOTO ©RANDALL K. ROBERTS

PAGE 44/45: The view from inside Landscape Arch, Devils Garden. PHOTO ©TOM TILL
NOTE: The trail from which this photograph was made is no longer open due to the danger of rock falls.

Turret Arch and Hale–Bopp Comet.   PHOTO ©TOM TILL

As the sun sets at the end of a hot summer's day in Arches, the rocks feel warm to the touch and seem to catch fire as the sinking sun catches their sculpted facades. As dusk draws in, the outlines of Delicate Arch, Fiery Furnace, Balanced Rock, and other landmarks begin to dissolve into enveloping darkness. A cool breeze blows through the sandy stone corridors. Venus, the evening star, is a beacon above the western horizon. One by one, other stars and planets appear, and then the moon, whose phosphorescent light seems to transform the rocks and fill them with pagan mystery. In the silence, without benefit of sight, sounds magnify. The torrid heat of the day recedes, and the desert comes back to life.

After staying cool in burrows or behind rocks during the day, the many nocturnal residents of Arches start to move around. At twilight, crickets begin a hypnotic refrain and bats swoop away from alcove roosts. Toads croak beside potholes and try to attract mates. Coyote packs erupt in a frenzy of doggy barking after cornering a cottontail in the blackbrush. Canyon mice and other rodents investigate campsites for leftovers, knocking against pots and pans like tiny invaders. Present but almost never seen are small gray foxes that steal quietly across the flats and mountain lions pursuing mule deer in the remotest parts of the park.

All this animal activity takes place under clear desert skies, where, on a typical night, you might see more than 6,000 stars and a large number of shooting stars. In 1997, photographers flocked to Arches to photograph the appearance of the Hale-Bopp comet, one of the brightest comets of the 20th century. Trapped in our timebound lives, there is something compelling about witnessing ephemeral events like this in a place like Arches, among 200-million-year-old rocks juxtaposed against skies that witnessed the birth of our planet.

We take for granted our night skies, but chemical and light pollution is so globally prevalent that only 10 percent of the world's population can even see the stars now. At Arches, commercial development north of Moab, along U.S. 191, is leading to increased light pollution as gas stations, hotels, and other businesses floodlight their properties to maintain the safety of customers. The National Park Service and the city of Moab are installing alternative solutions, such as downward-facing lights, in order to maintain dark skies over Arches.

OPPOSITE: The Moon seen through a small opening in the Windows Section. PHOTO ©GLENN VAN NIMWEGEN

Edward Abbey outside his home in Tucson, Arizona, 1987.

My role? I see myself as an entertainer.
I'm trying to write good books . . .
make people laugh, make them cry.
Provoke them, make them angry.
Make them think, if possible.

—Edward Abbey

In 1956 and 1957, iconoclastic writer Edward Abbey worked as a seasonal ranger in what was then Arches National Monument. During that time, Abbey occupied a government house trailer near Balanced Rock in the Windows section and was responsible for taking visitors' entrance fees, answering questions, giving campfire talks at the campground, and doing trash pickup once a week. "This is the most beautiful place on earth," he wrote on his first day at his new job.

While working at Arches, Abbey explored the backcountry and kept a journal. Ten years later, he transformed this material into a popular memoir, *Desert Solitaire: A Season in the Wilderness*. Although he wrote 20 other books, *Desert Solitaire* remains Abbey's masterpiece—a love letter to the desert and a rallying call to stop the growth of "industrial tourism" in our national parks.

Born in 1927 and raised on a farm in the tiny Appalachian community of Home, Pennsylvania, Abbey developed his love of nature early on. He began writing adventure stories as a child but also loved painting, drawing, and music. He fell in love with the Southwest while riding the rails as a young man. After a stint in the army in Europe, he moved west to attend the University of New Mexico, where he earned an undergraduate degree in 1951 and a master's in philosophy in 1959. A romantic at heart, Abbey had a weakness for women but felt tied down by domesticity. He was married five times and fathered four children. He was separated from his wife Rita while a ranger at Arches and later reconciled with her and moved to California. Abbey and his fifth wife, Clarke, eventually settled in Tucson, Arizona.

Edward Abbey inspired either love or hate in those who knew him. Friends and admirers delighted in his humor, word play, penchant for philosophical debate, camaraderie, and spirit of adventure. Several found themselves immortalized in Abbey's most popular novel, 1975's *The Monkey Wrench Gang*, which introduced four environmental "monkey wrenchers" intent on saving the West from overdevelopment by sabotaging huge government projects like Glen Canyon Dam. Although Abbey and his friends never owned to such illegal tactics, the *Monkey Wrench Gang* inspired the founding of EarthFirst!, which uses outrageous publicity stunts to draw attention to environmental issues. The environmental movement felt a huge loss when Edward Abbey died in 1989. At his request, he was buried under a pile of rocks in the Sonoran Desert at an undisclosed location. His fondest wish was that he would be reborn as a buzzard and haunt the skies above the desert.

OPPOSITE: Cliffrose and Balanced Rock. PHOTO ©TOM TILL

Mules ears.   PHOTO ©ELIZABETH BOEHM

Indian rice grass.   PHOTO ©GEORGE H.H. HUEY

Prickly pear cactus.   PHOTO ©ELIZABETH BOEHM

Arches is a high-desert steppe environment, with an elevation of 3,960 to 5,653 feet. Annual rainfall averages 8.5 inches. Trapped between mountain ranges, far from modifying ocean breezes, this exposed desert has summer temperatures that frequently hit 110 degrees Fahrenheit in summer, with temperatures at ground level even higher—often 125 degrees. Conversely, winter is frigid, with nighttime temperatures dropping below zero at night and only reaching the 20s in the day.

You would think that nothing could possibly grow in such an environment, but you'd be wrong. Arches supports nearly 500 species of vascular plants, each of which has evolved clever ways of adapting to this challenging habitat. Plants fall roughly into three types: drought resisters, drought escapers, and drought evaders.

Perennial woody-stemmed plants dominate the desert and are drought resisters (xerophytes). They have wide, shallow root systems or long taproots to quickly suck up rainwater when it arrives. The desert scrub and sand dune communities have many drought-resistant plants. Blackbrush, Russian thistle, and saltbush favor shallow sandy soils. Purple sage, old man sagebrush, fleabane, wild buckwheat, and sand verbena occupy the deeper sands that make up the sand dune community. Exposed desert scrub plants like Mormon tea cut down on evaporation by reducing the size of their leaves to tiny scales along joints and employing a waterproof waxy coating. Cacti, the desert's most adapted plants, have eliminated leaves altogether in favor of spines, which also protect them from predators. Their waxy pads and trunks can store large quantities of water to survive drought and are used instead of leaves to photosynthesize food from sunlight. Six species of cactus live in the park, including prickly pear, which produces flowers in spring and tasty fruits in summer.

Some plants are covered in fine white hairs to stay cool. Others have leaves that angle their leaves away from the sun. Some even drop their leaves completely during summer and lie dormant until the weather cools down. Mosses can completely dehydrate and spring back to life when it rains. Minerals in the soil also affect what will grow there. Four-wing saltbush, Mormon tea, pickleweed, greasewood, and shadscale (also known as sheep fat, an important forage for livestock) are adapted to saline soils such as those in Salt Valley. The uranium-laden Morrison and Chinle Formations are good places to view yellow-wanded princes plume and vetch, which need selenium.

The most common wildflowers in Arches are composite perennials of the sunflower family found in desert scrub. The flower head is not actually a single flower, but many. Bright composites like mules ears and blanketflower attract bees, which pollinate the flowers in spring. Some flowers have evolved to only bloom at night. Sword-leaved yucca has large white, fragrant flowers atop a spike that attract

Milkweed.   PHOTO ©ELIZABETH BOEHM

Cliffrose and Skyline Arch.   PHOTO ©LONDIE G. PADELSKY

Fragrand sand verbena.   PHOTO ©ELIZABETH BOEHM

Claret cup cactus. PHOTO ©STEVE MULLIGAN

Evening primrose. PHOTO ©GEORGE H.H. HUEY

Colorado four-o'clock. PHOTO ©ELIZABETH BOEHM

moths, which visit the flower in search of nectar and accidentally pollinate the plant. Other night bloomers include sacred datura, evening primrose, and sand verbena, part of the four o'clock family. In daytime, their flowers close up.

Pinyon and juniper woodland, which occupies nearly half of the park, is dominated by evergreen pinyon and juniper trees that sink roots into rocky soil and cracks between bedrock. Like many drought-resistant plants, pinyons and junipers are small but tough. Native people used the shaggy bark of the juniper as insulating material and harvested the highly nutritious nuts of the pinyon tree in fall. Pinyons and junipers are found in stands throughout Arches. This woodland is also home to 90 other plant species, including tough mountain mahogany, fragrant cliffrose, and deciduous wavy-leaf oak, which turns bronze and drops its leaves in fall.

Cottonwoods and willows are drought evaders and are the signature vegetation in riparian, or streamside, communities, such as Courthouse Wash, where the water table is close to the surface. Cottonwoods have thick furrowed trunks and aspen-like leaves that change hue to bright yellow in the fall, a beautiful counterpoint to the deep red branches of turning willows. Both trees are important habitat for birds, bats, and other creatures, which use them as nests and resting areas. Cottonwoods and willows are increasingly crowded out by nonnative tamarisk, or salt cedar, an introduced tree planted for erosion control. Exotic tamarisk reproduces faster than native trees, sucks up more water, tolerates salty conditions, forms dense thickets, and is rapidly turning western waterways into monocultural corridors.

Riparian areas are also home to a unique feature of Canyon Country: hanging gardens. Maidenhair fern, columbine, monkeyflower, bog orchid, and other moisture-loving plants find a home in cracks at the base of porous sandstone walls, where groundwater permeating the rock meets impervious shales and exits as springs. Although there is plenty of water here, these hanging gardens are among the most fragile of environments. Plants grow in soils created by collapsing walls and are slow to establish.

Native grasses like galleta, dropseed, and Indian ricegrass, which make up the grasslands community, are drought escapers, growing only when there is adequate rainfall in spring or late summer. These grasses are rapidly being crowded out by exotic cheatgrass, which reproduces while natives are dormant and takes over sandy swaled areas in grasslands. Annual wildflowers are also drought escapers. They lie dormant as seeds or bulbs in the soil, sometimes for years, waiting for adequate winter rainfall, then, when it comes, bloom in colorful waves. April and May in Arches offer spectacular shows of these ephemeral wildflowers. Check with the park to see what is blooming when you plan your trip.

Paintbrush. PHOTO ©GEORGE H.H. HUEY

Scarlet gilia. PHOTO ©GLENN VAN NIMWEGEN

Sweet pea. PHOTO ©SCOTT T. SMITH

PAGE 52/53: Cottonwoods in Courthouse Wash, autumn. PHOTO ©TOM TILL

Mule deer fawn. PHOTO ©GEORGE H.H. HUEY

Desert cottontail rabbit. PHOTO ©GEORGE H.H. HUEY

Bobcat (kitten). PHOTO ©GEORGE H.H. HUEY

Desert parks like Arches often seem rather austere and lifeless, especially in summer, when daytime heat keeps animals out of sight until the end of the day. But for the visitor who is willing to keep still and watch quietly, and most importantly, hike in the desert in the early morning or evening, when temperatures are cooler and most desert animals are active, there are huge rewards.

Most visible at any time of year are birds, which easily survive desert temperature extremes by flying from place to place. Large birds of prey cover huge distances, circling on thermals in search of prey. Look for the distinctive splayed red tail feathers of red-tailed hawks and the V-shaped profile of turkey vultures, or buzzards, patroling the skies. Park Avenue and Klondike Bluffs are home to hawks, eagles, and other birds of prey. One important denizen of the cliffs is the peregrine falcon—the fastest bird on earth, with speeds of 200 mph—which has made a comeback in the United States after near extinction. Peregrine falcons prey on white-throated swifts and often hassle even big birds like eagles.

Ubiquitous throughout Canyon Country are pairs of huge black ravens, which perch atop rocks, tree branches, fenceposts, and tent poles. These intelligent corvids communicate through as many as 30 different vocalizations, mainly, it seems, to do with how to steal food from campsites, picnic tables, and trash cans. Hikers often startle squawking scrub jays, titmice, and black-throated gray warblers in pinyon-juniper woodlands, where they are filling up on nuts before winter. Chirping blackthroated sparrows and fluting western meadowlarks are often seen in open grasslands. Listen carefully in rocky areas and you may hear a cascade of descending notes indicating the presence of a canyon wren, a rather drab little bird whose sweet song is a hallmark of Canyon Country.

Songbirds mainly concentrate along Courthouse Wash and the Colorado River, where sheltering cottonwoods, food, and water are plentiful. In spring and summer, look for blue grosbeaks, yellow-breasted chats, spotted towhees, dippers, and great blue herons fishing in the shallows. The birds feed on gnats, mosquitoes, deer flies, wasps, bees, and other insects, which hatch in May and can inflict a nasty bite just when temperatures are most perfect for hiking. The Colorado River contains some 14 species of fish, four of which are native and others introduced as sport fish. Native fish such as the Colorado squawfish are now extremely endangered. They evolved in the warmer waters of the pre-dammed river and are being outcompeted by cold-water-adapted fish like bass, catfish, and carp.

Arches has a surprising number of amphibians. Toads and frogs have all found a way to live here. Spadefoot, Woodhouse, and red-spotted toads are often encountered beside potholes, where they can dig themselves into the mud indefinitely to wait out drought. Once it rains,

Mountain lion. PHOTO ©TOM and PAT LEESON

Common raven. PHOTO ©SCOTT T. SMITH

Gray fox. PHOTO ©GEORGE H.H. HUEY

Badger.　PHOTO ©TOM and PAT LEESON

Kangaroo rat.　PHOTO ©GLENN VAN NIMWEGEN

Collared lizard.　PHOTO ©CAROL POLICH

they reemerge, and the males sing loudly to attract mates. Eggs hatch within hours, but metamorphosis, the transformation from tadpole to frog, takes several weeks. Survival depends on how much it rains and how long potholes stay full.

Arches has 20 species of reptiles, from small harmless side-blotched lizards and colorful collared lizards to poisonous midget-faded rattlesnakes. Since reptiles are cold-blooded, they cannot control body temperature and must avoid getting too hot or too cold. In summer, they can be seen basking in summer sunshine to warm up after cooler nighttime temperatures. When it is hottest, they shelter beneath rocks and bushes, only reappearing at twilight when the sun disappears. Reptiles survive winter cold by hibernating and living off accumulated fat stored in their bodies. Most snakes are nocturnal and harmless. Watch where you place your hands and feet on the trail. You're more likely to encounter lizards, which, when

startled, will push themselves up to seem bigger, either to scare you or to get a better look. Avoid picking up lizards. Their tails may detach in your hand, depriving them of an important winter food source while a new one is growing.

Reptiles are prey for some of the 50 mammal species in the park. Most are small mammals such as rodents that make homes in cool burrows and do well on the available food and water in this hot, dry desert. Watch for desert cottontails and the desert hare, known as a jackrabbit, which has huge ears that serve as both cooling system and antennae. Also common are antelope ground squirrels, which dash across trails and roads, feathery tails arched over their backs to keep cool. There are 11 species of mice and rats in Arches, most of them nocturnal. The long-legged kangaroo rat is uniquely adapted to the desert. It metabolizes all of its water from seeds and never needs to drink.

These small nocturnal rodents lead careful lives, timing their activities to avoid larger preda-

tors such as packs of coyotes and solitary gray foxes, which are crepuscular, meaning they are most active at twilight and dawn. Mule deer are also crepuscular and often travel for miles in search of water. They are the main diet of mountain lions, or cougars, whose large pawprints can sometimes be seen in remote areas next to heart-shaped deer tracks, though sightings of the big cats themselves are rare.

Much more visible but equally timid are desert bighorn sheep, which are making a comeback in Arches after being reintroduced from neighboring Canyonlands. Excellent climbers, desert bighorn prefer the talus slopes and side canyons near the Colorado River and are frequently sighted close to the visitor center along U.S. 191. Although the herd has grown to 75 animals, the number of lambs surviving their first year has decreased in recent years, perhaps due to increased vehicular traffic. Drive carefully along this stretch of the highway to avoid hitting any animals.

Porcupine and young.　PHOTO ©TOM and PAT LEESON

Least chipmunk.　PHOTO ©GEORGE H.H. HUEY

Side-blotched lizard.　PHOTO ©CAROL POLICH

Green River Overlook, Canyonlands National Park.
PHOTO © JEFF D. NICHOLAS

Independence Rock, Colorado National Monument.
PHOTO © TOM TILL

Late afternoon at Dead Horse Point State Park.
PHOTO © JEFF D. NICHOLAS

CANYONS OF THE ANCIENTS
NATIONAL MONUMENT

15 Burnett Court, Durango, CO 81301

Canyons of the Ancients National Monument adjoins Hovenweep National Monument on Cajon Mesa, 9 miles west of Mesa Verde National Park. Set aside in 2000, the 164,000-acre monument contains 20,000 archaeological sites, the highest known density anywhere in the United States. This is a remote undeveloped monument, managed by the BLM. It includes Lowry Pueblo, a 40-room stabilized pueblo with eight kivas and a great kiva, built about A.D. 1060 and abandoned in 1225.

CANYONLANDS
NATIONAL PARK

2282 S. West Resource Blvd., Moab, UT 84532

527-square-mile Canyonlands National Park sits directly south and southwest of Arches and preserves three distinct "districts" carved by the Colorado and Green Rivers. Island in the Sky is 32 miles west of Moab and, at 6,000 feet in elevation, offers an accessible overview of the Paradox Basin, along with easy day hikes, scenic drives, and Jeeping and mountain biking on 100-mile-long White Rim Trail. The 4,000-foot-elevation Needles District is 76 miles southwest of Moab and preserves lovely banded rock formations, grasslands, Ancestral Pueblo ruins, and cowboy camps. The Maze can only be reached via Utah 24, south of Green River, and is wild, remote country. Most accessible is the 30-mile sandy road to the Barrier Canyon rock art panel in Horseshoe Canyon. River outfitters in Moab also offer trips into Canyonlands.

COLORADO
NATIONAL MONUMENT

Fruita, CO 81521–0001

Rising 2,000 feet above the Grand Valley of the Colorado River, on the northeastern edge of the Uncompahgre Uplift, 20,453.93-acre Colorado National Monument protects towering red sandstone monoliths, deep, sheer-walled canyons, and wildlife found in pinyon-juniper woodlands. Hiking trails and 23-mile-long Rim Rock Drive offer expansive views to the Book Cliffs, northwest of Moab. Saddlehorn Campground has eight sites and is open all year; water seasonally.

DEAD HORSE POINT
STATE PARK

P.O. Box 609, Moab, UT 84532

Located next to the Island in the Sky District of Canyonlands, this 5,250-acre state park has breathtaking eastern views of the La Sal Mountains, eroded cliffs, mesas, buttes, and river canyons. At the base of the 2,000-foot mesa is an enormous horseshoe-shaped bend, or entrenched meander, in the Colorado River. Dead Horse Point itself is a sandstone peninsula separated by a 30-yard-wide "neck." According to legend, it was used as a corral by turn-of-the-century ranchers. On one occasion, for some forgotten reason, horses were left corralled here without water and died of thirst, hence the name. The park has 10 miles of rim trails and a 21-site campground with developed facilities.

DINOSAUR
NATIONAL MONUMENT

4545 E. Highway 40, Dinosaur, CO 81610

Some 1,600 dinosaur bones in more than 400 fossil sites are preserved in situ, embedded in a sheer wall in the Morrison Formation, at this 330-square-mile national monument, 20

OPPOSITE: North Window, Windows Section. PHOTO ©BRUCE HUCKO

Steamboat Rock, Echo Park, Dinosaur National Park.
PHOTO ©TOM TILL

Square Tower Group, Hovenweep National Monument.
PHOTO ©JEFF D. NICHOLAS

Owachomo Bridge, Natural Bridges National Monument.
PHOTO ©JEFF D. NICHOLAS

miles east of Vernal, Utah. Stegosaurus, Camptosaurus, Diplodocus, Camarasaurus, and Allosaurus are among the 10 kinds of dinosaurs on display. Activities include driving, hiking, and river running on the Green and the Yampa River, the last free-flowing river in the Colorado River System.

EDGE OF THE CEDARS
STATE PARK MUSEUM

600 West 400 North, Blanding, UT 84511

This not-to-be-missed cultural park preserves the remains of a major Ancestral Puebloan village and great kiva, dating from A.D. 825 to 1220. The museum serves as the archaeological repository for southeastern Utah and has modern research and artifact processing areas. A large quantity of prehistoric pottery uncovered in the area is housed here. Also notable is a rare ceremonial sash, made of scarlet macaw feathers, yucca fiber cords, and squirrel pelt, ca. A.D. 920-955, which was found in Lavender Canyon by legendary Canyonlands guide Kent Frost. State-of-the-art, multimedia exhibits interpret the prehistoric Ancestral Puebloan and modern Ute and Navajo cultures. There are native plant

and sculpture gardens and picnic areas, but no camping.

HOVENWEEP
NATIONAL MONUMENT

McElmo Route, Cortez, CO 81321

Six 12th- and 13th-century Mesa Verde-style Ancestral Pueblo buildings, built in unusual round, square, and D-shaped towers, line the rim of Little Ruin Canyon at this 1.2-square-mile national monument on Cajon Mesa, between Blanding, Utah, and Cortez, Colorado. Two short rim trails lead from a beautiful new visitor center and campground to Square Tower Group, Hovenweep Castle, and other structures used by prehistoric farmers.

NATURAL BRIDGES
NATIONAL MONUMENT

P.O. Box 1, Lake Powell, UT 84533

This 11.9-square-mile national monument, south of Canyonlands' Needles District, was the first to be set aside in Utah, in 1906. It preserves three dramatic Cedar Mesa Sandstone natural bridges carved by tributaries of the Colorado River. At 220 feet, Sipapu Bridge is second in size only to nearby Rainbow Bridge.

Visitors may hike canyon bottoms to view Sipapu, Kachina, and Owachomo Bridges. They can also be viewed from above on 9-mile Bridge View Drive, along with Horsecollar Ruin, a delightful 12th-century Ancestral Pueblo ruin that shows both Kayenta and Mesa Verde cultural influences. The 13-site campground is a treasure. The visitor center is housed in one of the first solar-powered buildings in the National Park System.

NEWSPAPER ROCK
STATE HISTORICAL MONUMENT

P.O. Box 788, Blanding, UT 84511

Newspaper Rock is a roadside rock art panel, 15 miles east of the Needles District of Canyonlands. It preserves 2,000 years of Ancestral Pueblo, Fremont, Ute, Navajo, and historic Anglo use of the area. Petroglyphs are carved into desert varnish, the dark, shiny patina found on sandstone walls through Canyon Country. No entrance fees or facilities. Camping is available at sheltered sites along Indian Creek.

OPPOSITE: Turret Arch seen through North Window, sunrise. PHOTO ©RANDY PRENTICE
PAGE 60/61: Early morning light on Broken Arch. PHOTO ©ROBERT HILDEBRAND

RESOURCES & INFORMATION

EMERGENCY AND MEDICAL
DIAL 911

ROAD CONDITIONS
(800) 492-2400

FOR MORE INFORMATION
NATIONAL PARKS ON THE INTERNET
www.nps.gov/

ARCHES NATIONAL PARK
PO Box 907
Moab, UT 84532
(435) 719-2299, (435) 719-2319 TTY
www.nps.gov/arch

CANYONLANDS NATURAL
HISTORY ASSOCIATION
3031 South Highway 191
Moab, UT 84532
(800) 840-8978, (435) 259-6003
www.cnha.org

MOAB INFORMATION CENTER
Center Street and Main
Moab, UT 84532
(435) 259-1370

BUREAU OF LAND
MANAGEMENT
www.ut.blm.gov/

CAMPING INSIDE
THE PARK
RESERVATIONS OFFICE
2282 South West Resource Blvd
Moab, UT 84532
(435) 259-4285 (Fax)

LODGING INSIDE
THE PARK
There are no accomodations
available within Arches National
Park.

LODGING OUTSIDE
THE PARK
GRAND COUNTY TRAVEL
COUNCIL
PO Box 550, Moab, UT 84532
(800) 635-MOAB

OTHER REGIONAL SITES
ANASAZI STATE PARK
PO Box 1429, Boulder, UT 84716
(435) 335-7308

AZTEC RUINS NATIONAL MONUMENT
84 County Road 2900
Aztec, NM 87410
(505) 334-6174
www.nps.gov/azru

BANDELIER NATIONAL MONUMENT
HCR 1, Box 1, Suite 15
Los Alamos, NM 87544
(505) 672-0343
www.nps.gov/band

BRYCE CANYON NATIONAL PARK
Bryce Canyon, UT 84717
(435) 834-5322
www.nps.gov/brca

CANYON OF THE ANCIENTS NATIONAL
MONUMENT
San Juan Public Lands Center
15 Burnett Court, Durango, CO 81301

(970) 247-4874, www.blm.gov/canm/
CANYONLANDS NATIONAL PARK
2282 South West Resource Blvd.
Moab, UT 84532
(435) 259-7164
www.nps.gov/cany

CAPITOL REEF NATIONAL PARK
Torrey, UT 84775
(435) 425-3791
www.nps.gov/care

CEDAR BREAKS NATIONAL MONUMENT
2390 West Highway 56, Suite 11
Cedar City, UT 84720
(435) 586-9451
www.nps.gov/cebr

CHACO CULTURE NATIONAL HISTORICAL PARK
PO Box 220, Nageezi, NM 87037
(505) 786-7014
www.nps.gov/chcu

COLORADO NATIONAL MONUMENT
Fruita, CO 81521
(970) 858-3617
www.nps.gov/colm

DEAD HORSE POINT STATE PARK
PO Box 609, Moab, UT 84532
(435) 259-2614, (800) 322-3770
(Camping Res.)

DINOSAUR NATIONAL
MONUMENT
4545 East Highway 40
Dinosaur, CO 81610-9724
(Visitor Center)
or
11625 East 1500 South
Jensen, UT 84035
(Carnegie Quarry)
(435) 789-2115 or (970) 374-3000
www.nps.gov/dino

EDGE OF THE CEDARS STATE
PARK MUSEUM
660 West 400 North
Blanding, UT 84533
(435) 678-2238

ESCALANTE STATE PARK
710 North Reservoir Road
Escalante, UT 84726
(435) 826-4466

FREMONT INDIAN STATE PARK
11550 West Clear Creek Canyon Road
Sevier, UT 84766
(435) 527-4631

GLEN CANYON NATIONAL
RECREATION AREA
PO Box 1507, Page, AZ 86040
(928) 608-6200
wwwnps.gov/glca

GOBLIN VALLEY STATE PARK
PO Box 637, Green River, UT 84525
(435) 564-3633

GOOSENECKS STATE PARK
PO Box 78, Blanding, UT 84511
(435) 678-2238

GREEN RIVER STATE PARK
PO Box 637, Green River, UT 84525
(435) 564-8882

HOVENWEEP NATIONAL MONUMENT
McElmo Route, Cortez, CO 81321
(970) 562-4284
www.nps.gov/hove

KODACHROME BASIN STATE PARK
PO Box 238, Cannonville, UT 84718
(435) 678-5622

ABOVE: Stream and pool in un-named canyon. PHOTO ©GLENN VAN NIMWEGEN

MESA VERDE NATIONAL PARK
PO Box 8
Mesa Verde National Park, CO 81330
(970) 529-4465, 529-4633 (TDD)
www.nps.gov/meve

NATURAL BRIDGES NATIONAL MONUMENT
HC 60, Box 1
Lake Powell, UT 84533
(435) 692-1234
www.nps.gov/nabr

NAVAJO NATIONAL MONUMENT
HC 71, Box 3
Tonalea, AZ 86044
(928) 672-2700
www.nps.gov/nava

NEWSPAPER ROCK STATE
HISTORICAL MONUMENT
PO Box 788
Blanding, UT 84511-0788
(435) 678-2238

PARASHANT NATIONAL
MONUMENT
601 Nevada Highway
Boulder City, NV 89005
(702) 293-8907
www.nps.gov/para

PETROGLYPH NATIONAL
MONUMENT
6001 Unser Blvd NW
Albuquerque, NM 87120
(505) 899-0205
www.nps.gov/petr

RAINBOW BRIDGE
NATIONAL MONUMENT
PO Box 1507
Page, AZ 86040
(928) 608-6404
www.nps.gov/rabr

UTAH STATE PARKS
1636 West North Temple
Salt Lake City, UT 84116
(801) 538-7720
www.parks.state.ut.us/parks/

ZION NATIONAL PARK
Springdale, UT 84767
(435) 772-3256,
www.nps.gov/zion

SUGGESTED READING

Abbey, Edward. *Desert Solitaire*. (1968). Reprint. New York, NY: Ballantine Books. 1971.

Baars, Donald L. *The Colorado Plateau: A Geologic History*. Revised Edition. Albuquerque, NM: University of New Mexico Press. 2000.

Canyon Legacy, The Journal of the Dan O'Laurie Canyon Country Museum. Winter 1998/Volume 34. "Ever-Changing Landscape: Arches National Park." Moab, Utah.

Chesher, Greer K. *Grand Staircase–Escalante National Monument: Heart of the Desert Wild*. Bryce Canyon, UT: Bryce Canyon Natural History Association. 2000.

Childs, Craig. *The Secret Knowledge of Water: Discovering the Essence of the American Desert*. Seattle, WA: Sasquatch Books. 2000.

Confessions of a Barbarian: Selections from the Journals of Edward Abbey, 1951-1989. Edited and with an introduction by David Petersen. Original drawing by Edward Abbey. New York: Little, Brown, and Company. 1994.

De Buys, William. *Seeing Things Whole: The Essential John Wesley Powell*. San Francisco, CA: Island Press. 2001.

Frost, Kent, with Rosalie Goldman. *My Canyonlands*. Monticello, UT: Canyon Country Publications. 1997.

Hinchman, Sandra. *Hiking the Southwest's Canyon Country*. Seattle, WA: The Mountaineers Books. 1997.

Hoffman, John F. *Arches National Park: An Illustrated Guide and History* (out of print; check Amazon.com). San Diego, CA: Western Recreational Publications. 1981.

Leach, Nicky. *Arches and Canyonlands National Parks. A Wish You Were Here Pocket Portfolio Book*. Mariposa, CA: Sierra Press. 1997.

_____. *The National Parks of Utah: A Journey to the Colorado Plateau*. Mariposa, CA: Sierra Press. 2002.

Lopez, Barry Holstun. *Desert Notes: Reflections in the Eye of a Raven*. New York, NY: Avon Books. 1976.

Melloy, Ellen. *Raven's Exile: A Season on the Green River*. New York, NY: Henry Holt. 1994.

Nabhan, Gary Paul, and Caroline Wilson. *Canyons of Color: Utah's Slickrock Wildlands*. San Diego, CA: Tehabi Books. 1995.

Nabhan, Gary Paul and Stephen Trimble. *The Geography of Childhood: Why Children Need Wild Places*. Boston, MA: Beacon Press. 1994.

Newell, Maxine. *A Story of Life at Wolfe Ranch*. Moab, UT: Canyonlands Natural History Association. 1995.

Rusho, W.L. *Everett Reuss: A Vagabond for Beauty*. Salt Lake City, UT: Gibbs Smith Publishers. 1983.

Tales of Canyonlands Cowboys. Edited by Richard F. Negri. Logan, UT: Utah State University Press. 1997

Thybony, Scott. *Canyon Country Parklands: Treasures of the Great Plateau*. Washington, D.C.: National Geographic Society. 1993.

Wilkinson, Charles. *Fire on the Plateau: Conflict and Endurance in the American Southwest*. San Francisco, CA: Island Press. 1999.

Williams, David. *A Naturalist's Guide to Canyon Country*. Helena, MT: Falcon Press in cooperation with Canyonlands Natural History Association. 2000.

Williams, Terry Tempest. *Red: Passion and Patience in the Desert*. New York: Pantheon Books. 2001.

ABOVE: Double Arch, Windows Section, early morning. PHOTO ©TOM TILL

PRODUCTION CREDITS

Publisher: Jeff D. Nicholas
Author: Nicky Leach
Editor: Cindy Bohn
Production Assistant: Melissa Wass
Illustrations: Darlece Cleveland
Printing Coordination: Sung In Printing America

ISBN 1-58071-051-4 (Cloth), 1-58071-50-6 (Paper)
©2003 Panorama International Productions, Inc.

Printed in the Republic of South Korea.
First printing, Spring 2003.

SIERRA PRESS

4988 Gold Leaf Drive, Mariposa, CA 95338
(209) 966-5071, 966-5073 (Fax)
e-mail: siepress@yosemite.net
VISIT OUR WEBSITE AT:
www.nationalparksusa.com

BELOW
Dry Mesa and sedges in Salt Wash.
PHOTO ©ROBERT HILDEBRAND
RIGHT
Early morning in the Courthouse Towers.
PHOTO ©CAROL POLICH
BACK COVER
Pothole in Park Avenue, late afternoon.
PHOTO ©JEFF D. NICHOLAS